Sherlock
100+ Facts on Sherlock and the Smash Hit BBC TV Series

By Andy Bell

As a "thank you" for purchasing this book I want to give you a gift. It is 100% absolutely free.

Please go to http://fandomkindlebooks.com/sherlock-bonus to discover more fascinating facts about Sherlock and the smash hit BBC TV series created exclusively for you.

Disclaimer

Photo credit: Fat Les

Table of Contents

Introduction

Sherlock Holmes is one of those iconic fictional characters who has come to life in the imaginations of all who have read the books, seen the films or waited with bated breath to follow the TV series.

Brought to life by Scottish author and physician Sir Arthur Conan Doyle, he first arrived in print in 1887. Since then he has been known the world over alongside his faithful sidekick Dr. Watson.

What has made Sherlock Holmes so popular over the years is hard to pinpoint. Perhaps it is his sense of logic, or that he solved his crimes in an era before technology took hold. Maybe it is because he just blends seamlessly across the generations, as much at home in 21st century London, as he would have been back in Victorian days.

The latest BBC offering is simply titled 'Sherlock' and has found a whole new legion of fans.

The series first aired in 2010 and sees a contemporary Sherlock tackling crimes with an array of modern gadgets and technology.

Written by Steven Moffat and Mark Gatiss, it is a sympathetic adaptation featuring many of the traditional elements and characters of the story. It weaves a spell of intrigue in a modern setting that enables the story to capture the imagination of its viewer just as the original stories did to their readers.

Come with me as I share facts and morsels of information that make up the world of 'Sherlock'.

Background of Sherlock Holmes

Film, Book Stage and TV

It is thought that Sherlock Holmes is the most prolific fictional character ever and the Guinness Book of Records maintains he is the most acted part in the history of film.

The Universal Sherlock Holmes (1995) written by Ronalf B DeWaal states there are over 25,000 Sherlock Holmes related productions and products.

More than 70 actors in over 200 films have portrayed the part of Sherlock Holmes.

There was a ballet called 'The Great Detective' that was based on Sherlock Holmes.

The first stage play based on Holmes was received in 1899 and written by William Gillette.

Books and stories based on Sherlock Holmes were the second biggest seller worldwide in 1964. The top spot was taken by the Bible.

One of the final scenes in the episode 'A Scandal in Belgravia took place in the midst of the London riots in 2011. The production team had been warned by Police that things could get heated so they rushed to get finished in time. As the scene was near completion, an assistant rushed in and shouted 'Go!' and everyone had to flee in order to get away from the riot.

Sir Arthur Conan Doyle

Doyle based the character of Holmes on his former university professor, Joseph Bell. Such was the likeness of character that Rudyard Kipling recognized him straight away declaring 'Is this my old friend, Dr. Joe?'

A pretty bad bout of influenza left Doyle fighting for his life. Once recovered he decided to dedicate his life to writing.

After writing so many books and short stories of Sherlock Holmes, Doyle grew tired and fed up of him. He considered killing him off and wrote to his mother in 1891 saying 'I think of slaying Holmes......and winding him up for good and all'. His mother tried to dissuade him as she thought the public would never forgive him. This proved to be true when he killed Holmes off at the end of 'The Final Problem'. Such was the outcry that he was forced to bring him back to life with a complicated explanation of what had happened. Holmes lived to fight another day.

Doyle always believed it was his writings on 'The War in South Africa: Its Cause and Conduct' that gained him his knighthood in 1902 and not his works on Holmes.

He tried to enlist in the army twice. He was declined both times.

The Making of the BBC series

The Writers and Production

The idea to create a contemporary adaptation of Sherlock Holmes came from two writers named Steven Moffat and Mark Gatiss. At the time they were writing on the Doctor Who series, which was being filmed in Cardiff, Wales. During long train journeys to and from London the idea for a modern day Holmes and Watson was conceived.

Writer Mark Gatiss is also an actor and appears as the character Mycroft, Holmes' brother, in Sherlock.

Writer Steven Moffat had this to say about the connection between Holmes and Doctor Who, 'Sherlock Holmes is a human that longs to be a god, The Doctor is a god that longs to be a human.'

The typeface used in the overlays is Johnston Sans, well-known for its use in the London Underground.

Matt Smith auditioned for the role of Doctor Watson before his Doctor Who audition.

The door knocker for 221B Baker Street is in a Victorian style that was popular around 1885. It has an aged brass finish.

Locations

Arguably the most popular of all the locations associated with Sherlock Holmes is his Baker Street address. The actual address used in filming is not Baker Street but in fact Flat 187, North Gower Street. During filming the door is removed and replaced with the famous 221B door.

St Bartholomew's hospital is the oldest hospital in London and the place where Sherlock and Dr. Watson first meet.

The senior members of the Metropolitan Police force 'live' at New Scotland Yard. It is also home to the Met's crime database, which, runs on a nationwide IT system called the 'Home Office Large Major Enquiry System' or HOLMES for short!

Officers learn how to use HOLMES via a software training program called 'ELEMENTARY.'

In the episode 'The Blind Banker' we see the fictitious financial institution of 'Shad Shanderson.' It is housed in Tower 42, which was originally built between 1971 and 1980. It used to house the international division of the NatWest Bank but now contains a mix of offices and restaurants. It once held the title of tallest building in London but now lies number 6 on the list.

Much of the filming for 'Sherlock' is done in Cardiff, Wales and integrated with the more well-known landmarks from London.

Connections between 'Sherlock' and 'Doctor Who'

The current series of both Doctor Who and Sherlock both shared writers Mark Gatiss and Steven Moffatt.

Sherlock and the Doctor have a great understanding of human nature, but are both somehow greatly removed from what is considered 'normal' human behavior.

They both surround themselves with sidekicks and companions who give them a sense of connection with other humans.

Doctor Who's arch nemesis 'The Master' has been likened to Moriarty, Sherlock's number one enemy.

Doctor Who and Sherlock are both quintessentially English and rather eccentric characters.

The fifth Doctor Who claimed to be a friend of Sherlock's.

The Doctor lived for a year at 107 Baker Street, making him almost a neighbor of Sherlock's at 221.

The second Doctor claimed to have met Sherlock.

The following actors have all appeared in Doctor Who and played the role of Sherlock Holmes:- Tom Baker, Nicholas Briggs, John Cleese, Peter Cushing, Jonathan Pryce and Roy Hued.

Both Doctor Who and Sherlock have enjoyed much popularity and longevity as British fictional characters in many different forms of media. They are both as popular and well-loved today as they have always been.

Fans

Fans reacted to the first episode of the third series of Sherlock by taking to Twitter with mixed reactions:

'Absolutely loved that. Great performances, wonderful script, but most of all loved that the makers had so much fun with it'

'#Sherlock. 90 mins of my life I'll never get back. BBC. You owe me.'

One set of Sherlock fans regularly make pilgrimages to the Reichenbach Falls where Sherlock originally met his untimely demise in 1891.

Sherlock fans are often known as 'Sherlockians.'

You know you're a Sherlockian when:

- You begin every game of Cluedo by shouting, 'the game Mrs. Hudson, is on.'

- You turn your collar up to look cool.

- You start twirling your umbrella and acting mysterious

Sherlock Jokes

Sherlock and Watson are on a camping trip. After a hearty supper and a good bottle of wine they retire to bed.

A few hours late, Holmes wakes and nudges his faithful friend.

'Watson' he asks, 'Look up at the sky and tell me what you see?'

Watson, looks up and replies 'I see millions and millions of stars.'

'And what does that tell you?' asks Holmes.

After much pondering Watson replies, 'Well, it tells me that there are millions of galaxies, and potentially billions of planets. It tells me that Saturn is in Leo. I deduce from the position of the stars that it is about three fifteen and that it will be a beautiful day tomorrow....what does is tell you Holmes?'

Holmes pauses for a while and then concludes 'That someone has stolen our tent Watson.'

Sherlock and Watson are walking around a rock museum.

Watson notices that there is a rock with no display name.

'I wonder what kind of rock that is?' he asks Holmes.

Holmes replies, 'Sedimentary, my dear Watson!'

Knock, knock.

Who's there?

Sherlock.

Sherlock who?

Sherlock your door shut tight.

Characters and Actors

Sherlock Holmes

Sherlock Holmes owned a Stradivarius violin, one of the most expensive violins in the world.

Sherlock uses a memory aiding technique that he calls 'Mind Palace.' This is not a fictitious method but rather one that dates back to ancient Rome. It works as a method of memory enhancement by using visualization to organize and recall information.

Sherlock was addicted to cocaine and morphine.

Holmes is a real life member of the Royal Society of Chemistry. He became the first fictional character, in 2002, to receive an Honorary Fellowship from the Society.

Sherlock believed in Spiritualism, fairies and ghosts. Something that he had in common with his creator Sir Arthur Conan Doyle.

Holmes has appeared on stamps in the following countries: the UK, Canada, South Africa, San Marino and Nicaragua.

Doyle's original name for Sherlock, as crossed out on a manuscript, was Sherrinford Holmes.

Benedict Cumberbatch (Sherlock)

Benedict was thorough in his preparation for the role of Holmes. Once cast he read every original Conan Doyle story.

During the summer of 2011 Danny Boyle created a production for the National Theatre of 'Frankenstein'. Benedict and Jonny Lee Miller played both the creator and monster, alternating the roles nightly. Both actors then went on to play Sherlock Holmes, albeit on opposite sides of the Atlantic.

Benedict's parents, Timothy Carlton and Wanda Ventham, were well-known TV actors when they had their son in the late 70s. They appear as Holmes' parents in the first episode of series 3.

As jobbing actors, the family regularly socialized with others in artistic circles, including Julian Fellowes, the writer and creator of Downton Abbey.

He was educated at top public school Harrow, although initially the school fees were considered to be outside the family's resources. However, after his then-headmaster recommended Harrow as a way to handle the riotously behaved Cumberbatch, he sat the entrance exam and gained a scholarship.

Benedict has appeared in Hollywood films, Tinker Tailor Soldier Spy, War Horse and The Hobbit. The latter also stars his co-star from Sherlock, Martin Freeman. Most recently he starred as Julian Assange in The Fifth Estate.

During his gap year, before studying at Manchester University, Benedict traveled to Tibet and taught English in a Tibetan Monastery.

Benedict considered turning down the role of Sherlock because of the attention it would bring. Mark Gatiss and Steven Moffat persuaded him to take the role on.

Una Stubbs, who plays Mrs. Hudson in Sherlock, is a close friend of his mother's and has watched Benedict grow up.

Benedict credits his co-star Martin Freeman for his dress sense. He used to be less than attentive to his appearance but Martin likes to wear good clothes, and Benedict says he has taken note, "He's a very natty dresser. He gets stuff made and is always coming in with new pairs of shoes so I've been watching his clobber..."

Dr. Watson

Dr. Watson narrates most of the Sherlock books.

Some sources place John Watson's birthdate as the 7th July 1852. The author himself died on the 7th July 1930.

Watson meets Sherlock after returning from the war and looking for lodgings. Sherlock becomes his new flat mate.

Dr. Watson is the name of a software program within MS Windows that detects, debugs and logs errors.

In Doyle's early plot outlines, Dr. Watson is named 'Ormond Sacker'. By the time the first book was published this was changed to the more familiar moniker, 'Dr. Watson.'

Watson's first name is only mentioned three times in the original books, but in the BBC series of Sherlock he is known by his first name John.

Martin Freeman (Dr. Watson)

Freeman's big break into acting came in 2001 when he was cast in 'The Office' created by Ricky Gervais.

He has featured in several big films, notably 'Love Actually' and more recently 'The Hobbit.'

Freeman takes the lead role in 'The Hobbit' with Benedict Cumberbatch narrating for the characters Smaug and The Necromancer.

Freeman was on the British National Squash Squad for 5 years from the age of 9.

Some Freeman quotes:

I've always got my eye on my deathbed. Will I be proud, or think I've sold out?

I love home, I'd rather be at home than anywhere else.

I would wear a full-length cape if I could get away with it – I do love a good swirl in the fog.

Freeman won a BAFTA for best supporting actor for his role as Dr. Watson in 2011.

Mrs. Hudson

Mrs. Hudson is the landlady of 221 Baker Street and not Sherlock's housekeeper.

She is a widow since her husband received the death penalty in Florida, something that Sherlock helps to ensure happens. A grateful Mrs. Hudson gives him a lower rent because of this.

It is not known what crime her husband committed but in episode 2 of series 3 Sherlock slips into a conversation with Mrs. Hudson that her husband was executed for double murder.

Whilst she puts up with a lot, she cannot abide Sherlock talking to his skull and regularly confiscates it.

In the original unaired pilot Mrs. Hudson owns Speedy's Café downstairs.

At first Mrs. Hudson assumes that John and Sherlock are a couple.

Although she repeatedly states that she is not his housekeeper, Mrs. Hudson fusses over Sherlock and they have a mother-son-like relationship.

Una Stubbs (Mrs. Hudson)

Attended the La Roche Dance School in Slough and began her career in the chorus line at The London Palladium at the age of 16.

She gets a lot of Chinese fan mail for her role as Mrs. Hudson. She saves the stamps and sends them off to her grandchildren.

She has said this of Sherlock actor Benedict Cumberbatch, 'There is nothing more unattractive than a man who thinks he is attractive. I think the fact that Benedict doesn't think he is attractive is so attractive to women.'

Her guilty pleasure is the TV series Big Brother.

Her first major role was in Cliff Richards 'Summer Holiday.'

Before Sherlock, she was best known for playing Rita in the sitcom Till Death Us Do Part and Aunt Sally in the series Worzel Gummidge.

Mycroft Holmes

Mycroft is seven years older than his brother Sherlock.

Although his powers of deduction are much stronger than those of Sherlock's, Mycroft hasn't the energy or desire to put them to good effect by doing detective work.

Mycroft loves his food and dines three times a day on three course meals each time.

Although he claims to have a 'minor position' within the British government, the fact he has access to high-level information and the power to manipulate computer systems, would indicate otherwise.

Sherlock often claims Mycroft 'is' the British government, when he is not working for the American CIA that is.

Mycroft was one of the founders, and is a member of, the gentlemen's club Diogenes. Members are not allowed to speak here for reasons of peace and quiet.

Despite the implied distance between the two brothers, Mycroft looks out for Sherlock, often warning Watson when Sherlock is in danger.

Mark Gatiss (Mycroft Holmes)

Mark is a talented all-rounder, a comedian, actor, screen writer and novelist.

His childhood dream was to write for Doctor Who.

Several wool tweed coats from Belstaff Milford are used in the filming of the series, but, the original one used in the pilot was bought by Mark and given to Benedict as a present.

Filming of The Hounds of Baskerville took place mostly as night shoots. One night Benedict inadvertently locked up the inn where the cast and crew were staying, not realizing that Mark and Sue Vertue (producer) weren't back. They were forced to spend the night sleeping in their car.

In the episode 'The Great Game' there is a scene with an elderly blind lady. The actress hadn't been given her lines beforehand, and so Mark hid at the bottom of her bed and gave her the lines as Moriarty to make the scene more authentic.

Benedict Cumberbatch was the only actor asked to audition for the role. Mark had worked with him on the film 'Starter for 10' and vouched for him.

Moriarty

Sherlock described Moriarty as the 'Napoleon of crime.'

Author Sir Arthur Conan Doyle based the character of Moriarty on Adam Worth an American criminal who came to England and built his network of crime in London.

Originally Moriarty only appeared in two of the Sherlock stories. However, over the years he has been given more prominence and climbed the ranks to become Sherlock's arch nemesis.

Dr. Watson never actually meets Moriarty, only hearing from him second hand through Sherlock.

Sherlock describes Moriarty as 'A man of good birth and excellent education. He is endowed with a phenomenal mathematical ability.'

Lestrade

The name Lestrade comes from Doyle's old university friend Joseph Alexandre Lestrad.

Lestrade is considered one of the best detectives at Scotland Yard, simply because Holmes lets him take the credit for his crime solving.

Lestrade has known Sherlock for five years.

Molly Hooper

Molly was originally going to be a one-off character used to introduce Sherlock. However, Louise Brealey (the actress who plays Molly) so impressed the writers that they couldn't resist bringing her back and now she is a regular character.

The character of Molly Hooper was not in the original Doyle books.

Mary Morstan

Actress Amanda Abbington, who plays the girlfriend and eventual wife of John Watson, is actually actor Martin Freeman's real life partner.

Mary dies in the original Doyle books, although her cause of death is never mentioned.

Irene Adler

In Irene, Sherlock meets his match. Every bit as brilliant as him, she is able to outwit him. However, her downfall is that she ends up falling in love with him.

The character of Irene Adler only appears in one of the original Doyle stories, but she has a big effect on Holmes and remains a significant character in his personal story.

Catch Phrases and quotes of Sherlock Holmes

'Elementary my dear Watson' – perhaps the most famous of all the catch phrases to come from Sherlock Holmes never actually appeared in the original stories. It is believed to have been added in a P.G Wodehouse film, Psmith Journalist in 1915.

'Come Watson, come. The game is afoot.'

'The plot thickens.'

'You know my methods Watson.'

Conclusion

The legacy of Sherlock Holmes continues to show no signs of abating.

With the BBC production of Sherlock now in its third series, new fans of Sherlock Holmes come on board every day.

A strange man seemingly at odds with most of his fellow humans, but with an unprecedented thirst for knowledge and logic, it doesn't seem possible that this is a character that was first written about 126 years ago.

Never before has literature seen a character as popular now as he was when he first came to people through the words on a page.

It is almost amusing that Doyle himself wanted to kill the character off because he grew bored of him. He could never have imagined that his popularity would have grown and grown as it has. Whatever would he think of the character he created now all these years later?

One can only hope he would now be proud that he created the most famous detective in the world.

Don't forget to claim your free gift!

As a "thank you" for purchasing this book I want to give you a gift. It is 100% absolutely free.

Please go to http://fandomkindlebooks.com/sherlock-bonus to discover more fascinating facts about Sherlock and the smash hit BBC TV series created exclusively for you.

Made in the USA
San Bernardino, CA
15 May 2014